MznLnx

Missing Links Exam Preps

Exam Prep for

Applied Calculus

Hughes-Hallett, et al., 2nd Edition

The MznLnx Exam Prep is your link from the texbook and lecture to your exams.
The MznLnx Exam Preps are unauthorized and comprehensive reviews of your textbooks.

All material provided by MznLnx and Rico Publications (c) 2010
Textbook publishers and textbook authors do not particpate in or contribute to these reviews.

MznLnx

Rico Publications

Exam Prep for Applied Calculus
2nd Edition
Hughes-Hallett, et al.

Publisher: Raymond Houge
Assistant Editor: Michael Rouger
Text and Cover Designer: Lisa Buckner
Marketing Manager: Sara Swagger
Project Manager, Editorial Production: Jerry Emerson
Art Director: Vernon Lowerui

Product Manager: Dave Mason
Editorial Assitant: Rachel Guzmanji
Pedagogy: Debra Long
Cover Image: Jim Reed/Getty Images
Text and Cover Printer: City Printing, Inc.
Compositor: Media Mix, Inc.

(c) 2010 Rico Publications
ALL RIGHTS RESERVED. No part of this work covered by the copyright may be reproduced or used in any form or by an means--graphic, electronic, or mechanical, including photocopying, recording, taping, Web distribution, information storage, and retrieval systems, or in any other manner--without the written permission of the publisher.

Printed in the United States
ISBN:

For more information about our products, contact us at:
Dave.Mason@RicoPublications.com

For permission to use material from this text or product, submit a request online to:
Dave.Mason@RicoPublications.com

Contents

CHAPTER 1
FUNCTIONS AND CHANGE — 1

CHAPTER 2
RATE OF CHANGE: THE DERIVATIVE — 14

CHAPTER 3
SHORT-CUTS TO DIFFERENTIATION — 21

CHAPTER 4
USING THE DERIVATIVE — 27

CHAPTER 5
ACCUMULATED CHANGE: THE DEFINITE INTEGRAL — 33

CHAPTER 6
USING THE DEFINITE INTEGRAL — 38

CHAPTER 7
ANTIDERIVATIVES — 39

CHAPTER 8
PROBABILITY — 45

CHAPTER 9
FUNCTIONS OF SEVERAL VARIABLES — 47

CHAPTER 10
MATHEMATICAL MODELING USING DIFFERENTIAL EQUATIONS — 56

CHAPTER 11
GEOMETRIC SERIES — 63

ANSWER KEY — 66

TO THE STUDENT

COMPREHENSIVE

The *MznLnx* Exam Prep series is designed to help you pass your exams. Editors at MznLnx review your textbooks and then prepare these practice exams to help you master the textbook material. Unlike study guides, workbooks, and practice tests provided by the texbook publisher and textbook authors, *MznLnx* gives you **all** of the material in each chapter in exam form, not just samples, so you can be sure to nail your exam.

MECHANICAL

The MznLnx Exam Prep series creates exams that will help you learn the subject matter as well as test you on your understanding. Each question is designed to help you master the concept. Just working through the exams, you gain an understanding of the subject--its a simple mechanical process that produces success.

INTEGRATED STUDY GUIDE AND REVIEW

MznLnx is not just a set of exams designed to test you, its also a comprehensive review of the subject content. Each exam question is also a review of the concept, making sure that you will get the answer correct without having to go to other sources of material. You learn as you go! Its the easiest way to pass an exam.

HUMOR

Studying can be tedious and dry. MznLnx's instructional design includes moderate humor within the exam questions on occassion, to break the tedium and revitalize the brain

Chapter 1. FUNCTIONS AND CHANGE

1. In economics, the _____ functional form of production functions is widely used to represent the relationship of an output to inputs. It was proposed by Knut Wicksell (1851-1926), and tested against statistical evidence by Charles Cobb and Paul Douglas in 1900-1928.

For production, the function is

$$Y = AL^{\alpha}K^{\beta},$$

where:

- Y = total production (the monetary value of all goods produced in a year)
- L = labor input
- K = capital input
- A = total factor productivity
- α and β are the output elasticities of labor and capital, respectively. These values are constants determined by available technology.

Output elasticity measures the responsiveness of output to a change in levels of either labor or capital used in production, ceteris paribus. For example if $\alpha = 0.15$, a 1% increase in labor would lead to approximately a 0.15% increase in output.

a. BIBO stability
b. Cobb-Douglas
c. 15 theorem
d. BDDC

2. The terms '_____' and 'independent variable' are used in similar but subtly different ways in mathematics and statistics as part of the standard terminology in those subjects. They are used to distinguish between two types of quantities being considered, separating them into those available at the start of a process and those being created by it, where the latter (dependent variables) are dependent on the former (independent variables.)

In traditional calculus, a function is defined as a relation between two terms called variables because their values vary.

a. Dependent variable
b. BIBO stability
c. 15 theorem
d. BDDC

Chapter 1. FUNCTIONS AND CHANGE

3. In mathematics, the _____ (or replacement set) of a given function is the set of 'input' values for which the function is defined. For instance, the _____ of cosine would be all real numbers, while the _____ of the square root would be only numbers greater than or equal to 0 (ignoring complex numbers in both cases.) In a representation of a function in a xy Cartesian coordinate system, the _____ is represented on the x axis (or abscissa.)
    a. Domain
    b. 15 theorem
    c. BIBO stability
    d. BDDC

4. The terms 'dependent variable' and '_____' are used in similar but subtly different ways in mathematics and statistics as part of the standard terminology in those subjects. They are used to distinguish between two types of quantities being considered, separating them into those available at the start of a process and those being created by it, where the latter (dependent variables) are dependent on the former (independent variables.)

    In traditional calculus, a function is defined as a relation between two terms called variables because their values vary.

    a. AUSM
    b. Independent variable
    c. ACTRAN
    d. ALGOR

5. In mathematics, the _____ of a function is the set of all 'output' values produced by that function. Sometimes it is called the image, or more precisely, the image of the domain of the function. If a function is a surjection then its _____ is equal to its codomain.
    a. Piecewise-defined function
    b. Constant function
    c. Surjective
    d. Range

6. Integration is an important concept in mathematics, specifically in the field of calculus and, more broadly, mathematical analysis. Given a function f of a real variable x and an interval [a, b] of the real line, the _____

$$\int_a^b f(x)\,dx,$$

is defined informally to be the net signed area of the region in the xy-plane bounded by the graph of f, the x-axis, and the vertical lines x = a and x = b.

The term '_____' may also refer to the notion of antiderivative, a function F whose derivative is the given function f.

   a. Integrand
   b. Integral test for convergence
   c. Integral
   d. Indefinite integral

7. In mathematics, a _____ is a function which preserves the given order. This concept first arose in calculus, and was later generalized to the more abstract setting of order theory.

In calculus, a function f defined on a subset of the real numbers with real values is called monotonic (also monotonically increasing or non-decreasing), if for all x and y such that x >≤ y one has f(x) >≤ f(y), so f preserves the order.

   a. 15 theorem
   b. Monotonic function
   c. Pseudo-differential operator
   d. Pettis integral

8. In mathematics, _____ is the process of constructing new data points outside a discrete set of known data points. It is similar to the process of interpolation, which constructs new points between known points, but the results of extrapolations are often less meaningful, and are subject to greater uncertainty. Example illustration of the _____ problem, consisting of assigning a meaningful value at the blue box, at x = 7, given the red data points.

A sound choice of which _____ method to apply relies on a prior knowledge of the process that created the existing data points.

   a. AUSM
   b. Extrapolation
   c. ACTRAN
   d. ALGOR

9. The function difference divided by the point difference is known as the _____, it is also known as Newton's quotient):

Chapter 1. FUNCTIONS AND CHANGE

$$\frac{\Delta F(P)}{\Delta P} = \frac{F(P + \Delta P) - F(P)}{\Delta P} = \frac{\nabla F(P + \Delta P)}{\Delta P}.$$

If ΔP is infinitesimal, then the _____ is a derivative, otherwise it is a divided difference:

$$\text{If } |\Delta P| = iota : \quad \frac{\Delta F(P)}{\Delta P} = \frac{dF(P)}{dP} = F'(P) = G(P);$$

$$\text{If } |\Delta P| > iota : \quad \frac{\Delta F(P)}{\Delta P} = \frac{DF(P)}{DP} = F[P, P + \Delta P].$$

Regardless if ΔP is infinitesimal or finite, there is (at least--in the case of the derivative--theoretically) a point range, where the boundaries are P ± (.5)ΔP (depending on the orientation--ΔF(P), δF(P) or ∇F(P)):

    LB = Lower Boundary; UB = Upper Boundary;

Anyone familiar with derivatives knows that they can be regarded as functions themselves, harboring their own derivatives. Thus each function is home to sequential degrees ('higher orders') of derivation, or differentiation. This property can be generalized to all difference quotients.As this sequencing requires a corresponding boundary splintering, it is practical to break up the point range into smaller, equi-sized sections, with each section being marked by an intermediary point ('P_i'), where LB = P_0 and UB = P_{A_n}, the nth point, equaling the degree/order:

LB = P_0 = P_0 + 0Δ_1P = P_{A_n} - (Åf-0)Δ_1P; P_1 = P_0 + 1Δ_1P = P_{A_n} - (Åf-1)Δ_1P; P_2 = P_0 + 2Δ_1P = P_{A_n} - (Åf-2)Δ_1P; P_3 = P_0 + 3Δ_1P = P_{A_n} - (Åf-3)Δ_1P; ↓↓↓↓ P_{A_n-3} = P_0 + (Åf-3)Δ_1P = P_{A_n} - 3Δ_1P; P_{A_n-2} = P_0 + (Åf-2)Δ_1P = P_{A_n} - 2Δ_1P; P_{A_n-1} = P_0 + (Åf-1)Δ_1P = P_{A_n} - 1Δ_1P; UB = P_{A_n-0} = P_0 + (Åf-0)Δ_1P = P_{A_n} - 0Δ_1P = P_{A_n};

ΔP = Δ_1P = P_1 - P_0 = P_2 - P_1 = P_3 - P_2 = ...

    a. Checkpointing schemes
    b. Linear approximation
    c. Point of inflection
    d. Difference quotient

10.   A _____ is an algebraic equation in which each term is either a constant or the product of a constant and (the first power of) a single variable. Linear equations can have one, two, three or more variables. Linear equations occur with great regularity in applied mathematics.

a. 15 theorem
b. BDDC
c. Cubic function
d. Linear equation

11. In calculus, an _____, primitive or indefinite integral of a function f is a function F whose derivative is equal to f, i.e., F >' = f. The process of solving for antiderivatives is antidifferentiation (or indefinite integration.) Antiderivatives are related to definite integrals through the fundamental theorem of calculus: the definite integral of a function over an interval is equal to the difference between the values of an _____ evaluated at the endpoints of the interval.

a. Indefinite integral
b. Order of integration
c. Antiderivative
d. Integrand

12. A _____ of a curve is a line that (locally) intersects two points on the curve. The word secant comes from the Latin secare, for to cut.

It can be used to approximate the tangent to a curve, at some point P. If the secant to a curve is defined by two points, P and Q, with P fixed and Q variable, as Q approaches P along the curve, the direction of the secant approaches that of the tangent at P, assuming there is just one.

a. Kappa curve
b. Witch of Agnesi
c. Curve
d. Secant line

13. In physics, _____ is defined as the rate of change of position. it is vector physical quantity; both speed and direction are required to define it. In the SI (metric) system, it is measured in meters per second: (m/s) or ms^{-1}.

a. BIBO stability
b. Velocity
c. BDDC
d. 15 theorem

14. In mathematics, the simplest case of _____ refers to the study of problems in which one seeks to minimize or maximize a real function by systematically choosing the values of real or integer variables from within an allowed set. This (a scalar real valued objective function) is actually a small subset of this field which comprises a large area of applied mathematics and generalizes to study of means to obtain 'best available' values of some objective function given a defined domain where the elaboration is on the types of functions and the conditions and nature of the objects in the problem domain.

The first _____ technique, which is known as steepest descent, goes back to Gauss.

a. ACTRAN
b. AUSM
c. ALGOR
d. Optimization

15. The _____ of a material is defined as its mass per unit volume. The symbol of _____ is ρ '>rho.)

Mathematically:

$$d = \frac{m}{V}$$

where:

d is the _____,
m is the mass,
V is the volume.

a. BIBO stability
b. Density
c. 15 theorem
d. BDDC

16. In mathematics, a (topological) _____ is defined as follows: let I be an interval of real numbers (i.e. a non-empty connected subset of $\mathbb{R}$); then a _____ γ is a continuous mapping $\gamma : I \to X$, where X is a topological space. The _____ γ is said to be simple if it is injective, i.e. if for all x, y in I, we have $\gamma(x) = \gamma(y) \implies x = y$. If I is a closed bounded interval $[a, b]$, we also allow the possibility $\gamma(a) = \gamma(b)$ (this convention makes it possible to talk about closed simple _____.)

a. Prolate cycloid
b. Closed curve
c. Tractrix
d. Curve

17. In mathematics, the point $\tilde{\mathbf{x}} \in \mathbb{R}^n$ is an _____ for the differential equation

$$\frac{d\mathbf{x}}{dt} = \mathbf{f}(t, \mathbf{x})$$

if $\mathbf{f}(t, \tilde{\mathbf{x}}) = 0$ for all t.

Similarly, the point $\tilde{\mathbf{x}} \in \mathbb{R}^n$ is an _____ (or fixed point) for the difference equation

$$\mathbf{x}_{k+1} = \mathbf{f}(k, \mathbf{x}_k)$$

if $\mathbf{f}(k, \tilde{\mathbf{x}}) = \tilde{\mathbf{x}}$ for $k = 0, 1, 2, \ldots$.

Equilibria can be classified by looking at the signs of the eigenvalues of the linearization of the equations about the equilibria.

a. Equilibrium point
b. AUSM
c. ACTRAN
d. ALGOR

18. In mathematics, an _____ is a generalization for the concept of a function in which the dependent variable has not been given 'explicitly' in terms of the independent variable. To give a function f explicitly is to provide a prescription for determining the output value of the function y in terms of the input value x:

y = f(x.)

By contrast, the function is implicit if the value of y is obtained from x by solving an equation of the form:

R(x,y) = 0.

a. Implicit differentiation
b. Automatic differentiation
c. Ordinary differential equation
d. Implicit function

19. The _____ is a function in mathematics. The application of this function to a value x is written as exp(x). Equivalently, this can be written in the form e^x, where e is a mathematical constant, the base of the natural logarithm, which equals approximately 2.718281828, and is also known as Euler's number.

a. ACTRAN
b. Area hyperbolic functions
c. Integral part
d. Exponential function

20. _____ (including exponential decay) occurs when the growth rate of a mathematical function is proportional to the function's current value. In the case of a discrete domain of definition with equal intervals it is also called geometric growth or geometric decay (the function values form a geometric progression.)

_____ is said to follow an exponential law; the simple-_____ model is known as the Malthusian growth model.

a. Inseparable differential equation
b. Isomonodromic deformation
c. Oscillating
d. Exponential growth

21. An _____ of a real-valued function y = f(x) is a curve which describes the behavior of f as either x or y tends to infinity.

In other words, as one moves along the graph of f(x) in some direction, the distance between it and the _____ eventually becomes smaller than any distance that one may specify.

a. AUSM
b. ALGOR
c. ACTRAN
d. Asymptote

22. Suppose f is a function. Then the line y = a is a _____ for f if

$$\lim_{x \to \infty} f(x) = a \text{ or } \lim_{x \to -\infty} f(x) = a.$$

Intuitively, this means that f(x) can be made as close as desired to a by making x big enough. How big is big enough depends on how close one wishes to make f(x) to a.

a. Bounded function
b. Horizontal asymptote
c. Mountain pass theorem
d. Vertical asymptote

23. A quantity is said to be subject to _____ if it decreases at a rate proportional to its value. Symbolically, this can be expressed as the following differential equation, where N is the quantity and λ is a positive number called the decay constant.

$$\frac{dN}{dt} = -\lambda N.$$

The solution to this equation is:

$$N(t) = N_0 e^{-\lambda t}.$$

Here N(t) is the quantity at time t, and N_0 = N(0) is the initial quantity, i.e. the quantity at time t = 0.

a. ACTRAN
b. ALGOR
c. Exponential sum
d. Exponential decay

24. _____ is the concept of adding accumulated interest back to the principal, so that interest is earned on interest from that moment on. The act of declaring interest to be principal is called compounding (i.e., interest is compounded.) A loan, for example, may have its interest compounded every month: in this case, a loan with $100 principal and 1% interest per month would have a balance of $101 at the end of the first month.
a. BIBO stability
b. 15 theorem
c. BDDC
d. Compound interest

Chapter 1. FUNCTIONS AND CHANGE

25. The _____ of a quantity whose value decreases with time is the interval required for the quantity to decay to half of its initial value. The concept originated in describing how long it takes atoms to undergo radioactive decay but also applies in a wide variety of other situations.

The term '_____' dates to 1907.

a. BDDC
b. Half-life
c. 15 theorem
d. BIBO stability

26. In mathematics, a _____ represents the application of one function to the results of another. For instance, the functions f: X → Y and g: Y → Z can be composed by first computing f(x) and then applying a function g to the output of f(x.)

Thus one obtains a function g ∘ f: X → Z defined by (g ∘ f)(x) = g(f(x)) for all x in X. The notation g ∘ f is read as 'g circle f', or 'g composed with f', 'g after f', 'g following f', or just 'g of f'.

a. Constant function
b. Surjective
c. Range
d. Composite function

27. is called the proportionality constant or _____.

- If an object travels at a constant speed, then the distance traveled is proportional to the time spent travelling, with the speed being the _____.

- The circumference of a circle is proportional to its diameter, with the _____ equal to π.

- On a map drawn to scale, the distance between any two points on the map is proportional to the distance between the two locations that the points represent, with the _____ being the scale of the map.

- The force acting on a certain object due to gravity is proportional to the object's mass; the _____ between the the mass and the force is known as gravitational acceleration.

Since

$$y = kx$$

is equivalent to

$$x = \left(\frac{1}{k}\right)y,$$

it follows that if y is proportional to x, with (nonzero) proportionality constant k, then x is also proportional to y with proportionality constant 1/k.

If y is proportional to x, then the graph of y as a function of x will be a straight line passing through the origin with the slope of the line equal to the _____ : it corresponds to linear growth.

a. 15 theorem
b. BIBO stability
c. BDDC
d. Constant of proportionality

28. In mathematics, a _____ is a constant multiplicative factor of a certain object. For example, in the expression $9x^2$, the _____ of x^2 is 9.

The object can be such things as a variable, a vector, a function, etc.

a. Degree of the polynomial
b. Coefficient
c. Leading coefficient
d. Difference polynomial

29. For the largest k where $a_k \neq 0$, a_k is called the _____ of P because most often, polynomials are written starting from the left with the largest power of x. So for example the _____ of the polynomial

$$4x^5 + x^3 + 2x^2$$

is 4.

The coefficients of polynomial also may be in the other order:

$$Q(x) = a_0 x^k + a_1 x^{k-1} + \cdots + a_{k-1} x^1 + a_k$$

and must be $a_0 \neq 0$ and a_0 is the _____ of Q.

Chapter 1. FUNCTIONS AND CHANGE

a. Constant term
b. Binomial type
c. Resultant
d. Leading coefficient

30. In mathematics, a _____ is a function that repeats its values in regular intervals or periods. The most important examples are the trigonometric functions, which repeat over intervals of length 2π. Periodic functions are used throughout science to describe oscillations, waves, and other phenomena that exhibit periodicity.
    a. Test for Divergence
    b. Nth term
    c. Term test
    d. Periodic function

31. In statistics, _____ is a form of regression analysis in which the relationship between one or more independent variables and another variable, called dependent variable, is modeled by a least squares function, called _____ equation. This function is a linear combination of one or more model parameters, called regression coefficients. A _____ equation with one independent variable represents a straight line.
    a. Standard deviation
    b. Poisson distribution
    c. Normal distribution
    d. Linear regression

32. In the mathematical subfield of numerical analysis, _____ is a method of constructing new data points within the range of a discrete set of known data points.

    In engineering and science one often has a number of data points, as obtained by sampling or experimentation, and tries to construct a function which closely fits those data points. This is called curve fitting or regression analysis.

    a. ACTRAN
    b. ALGOR
    c. Interpolation
    d. AUSM

33. The method of _____ or ordinary _____ is used to solve overdetermined systems. _____ is often applied in statistical contexts, particularly regression analysis.

Chapter 1. FUNCTIONS AND CHANGE

_____ can be interpreted as a method of fitting data. The best fit in the _____ sense is that instance of the model for which the sum of squared residuals has its least value, a residual being the difference between an observed value and the value given by the model.

a. 15 theorem
b. BDDC
c. Least squares
d. BIBO stability

34. In mathematics, the concept of a '_____' is used to describe the behavior of a function as its argument or input either 'gets close' to some point, or as the argument becomes arbitrarily large; or the behavior of a sequence's elements as their index increases indefinitely. Limits are used in calculus and other branches of mathematical analysis to define derivatives and continuity.

In formulas, _____ is usually abbreviated as lim

a. BDDC
b. BIBO stability
c. 15 theorem
d. Limit

Chapter 2. RATE OF CHANGE: THE DERIVATIVE

1. In calculus, a branch of mathematics, the _____ is a measurement of how a function changes when its input changes. Loosely speaking, a _____ can be thought of as how much a quantity is changing at some given point. For example, the _____ of the position (or distance) of a vehicle with respect to time is the instantaneous velocity (respectively, instantaneous speed) at which the vehicle is traveling.

The process of finding a _____ is called differentiation. The fundamental theorem of calculus states that differentiation is the reverse process to integration.

   a. Mountain pass theorem
   b. Ramp function
   c. Concave upwards
   d. Derivative

2. In calculus, _____, was originally the use of expressions such as dx and dy and to represent 'infinitely small' (or infinitesimal) increments of quantities x and y, just as >Δx and >Δy represent finite increments of x and y respectively. So for y being a function of x, or

> [x]>

the derivative of y with respect to x, which later came to be viewed as

> [x]>

was, according to Leibniz, the quotient of an infinitesimal increment of y by an infinitesimal increment of x, or

> [x]>

where the right hand side is Lagrange's notation for the derivative of f at x.

Similarly, although mathematicians usually now view an integral

> [x]>

as a limit

> [x]>

where >Δx is an interval containing x_i, Leibniz viewed it as the sum (the integral sign denoting summation) of infinitely many infinitesimal quantities f(x) dx.

Chapter 2. RATE OF CHANGE: THE DERIVATIVE

a. Notation for differentiation
b. Fermat differentiation
c. Leibniz's notation
d. Gradient

3. In geometry, the _____ (or simply the tangent) to a curve at a given point is the straight line that 'just touches' the curve at that point (in the sense explained more precisely below.) As it passes through the point of tangency, the _____ is 'going in the same direction' as the curve, and in this sense it is the best straight-line approximation to the curve at that point. The same definition applies to space curves and curves in n-dimensional Euclidean space.
    a. Minimal surface
    b. Sphere
    c. Lie derivative
    d. Tangent line

4. In mathematics, a (topological) _____ is defined as follows: let I be an interval of real numbers (i.e. a non-empty connected subset of $\mathbb{R}$); then a _____ γ is a continuous mapping $\gamma : I \to X$, where X is a topological space. The _____ γ is said to be simple if it is injective, i.e. if for all x, y in I, we have $\gamma(x) = \gamma(y) \implies x = y$. If I is a closed bounded interval $[a, b]$, we also allow the possibility $\gamma(a) = \gamma(b)$ (this convention makes it possible to talk about closed simple _____.)
    a. Closed curve
    b. Prolate cycloid
    c. Tractrix
    d. Curve

5. Let f be a differentiable function, and let f'(x) be its derivative. The derivative of f'(x) (if it has one) is written f''(x) and is called the _____ of f. Similarly, the derivative of a _____, if it exists, is written f'''(x) and is called the third derivative of f.
    a. Second derivative
    b. Ramp function
    c. Horizontal asymptote
    d. Stationary phase approximation

6. In economics, the _____ functional form of production functions is widely used to represent the relationship of an output to inputs. It was proposed by Knut Wicksell (1851-1926), and tested against statistical evidence by Charles Cobb and Paul Douglas in 1900-1928.

For production, the function is

$$Y = AL^{\alpha}K^{\beta},$$

where:

- Y = total production (the monetary value of all goods produced in a year)
- L = labor input
- K = capital input
- A = total factor productivity
- α and β are the output elasticities of labor and capital, respectively. These values are constants determined by available technology.

Output elasticity measures the responsiveness of output to a change in levels of either labor or capital used in production, ceteris paribus. For example if α = 0.15, a 1% increase in labor would lead to approximately a 0.15% increase in output.

   a. BIBO stability
   b. BDDC
   c. 15 theorem
   d. Cobb-Douglas

7. In mathematics, a _____ is a function whose values do not vary and thus are constant. For example, if we have the function f(x) = 4, then f is constant since f maps any value to 4. More formally, a function f : A → B is a _____ if f(x) = f(y) for all x and y in A.
   a. Piecewise-defined function
   b. Surjective
   c. Range
   d. Constant function

8. In mathematics, a _____ is a function which preserves the given order. This concept first arose in calculus, and was later generalized to the more abstract setting of order theory.

In calculus, a function f defined on a subset of the real numbers with real values is called monotonic (also monotonically increasing or non-decreasing), if for all x and y such that x >≤ y one has f(x) >≤ f(y), so f preserves the order.

a. Pettis integral
b. Pseudo-differential operator
c. 15 theorem
d. Monotonic function

9. If a function has an integral, it is said to be integrable. The function for which the integral is calculated is called the _____. The region over which a function is being integrated is called the domain of integration.
   a. Order of integration
   b. Integration by parts
   c. Integral test for convergence
   d. Integrand

10. Integration is an important concept in mathematics, specifically in the field of calculus and, more broadly, mathematical analysis. Given a function f of a real variable x and an interval [a, b] of the real line, the _____

$$\int_a^b f(x)\, dx,$$

is defined informally to be the net signed area of the region in the xy-plane bounded by the graph of f, the x-axis, and the vertical lines x = a and x = b.

The term '_____' may also refer to the notion of antiderivative, a function F whose derivative is the given function f.

   a. Indefinite integral
   b. Integral test for convergence
   c. Integrand
   d. Integral

11. In physics, and more specifically kinematics, _____ is the change in velocity over time. Because velocity is a vector, it can change in two ways: a change in magnitude and/or a change in direction. In one dimension, _____ is the rate at which something speeds up or slows down.
   a. ACTRAN
   b. AUSM
   c. ALGOR
   d. Acceleration

Chapter 2. RATE OF CHANGE: THE DERIVATIVE

12. In mathematics, a _____ is an approximation of a general function using a linear function (more precisely, an affine function.)

Given a differentiable function f of one real variable, Taylor's theorem for n=1 states that

$$f(x) = f(a) + f\,'(a)(x-a) + R_2$$

where R_2 is the remainder term. The _____ is obtained by dropping the remainder:

$$f(x) \approx f(a) + f\,'(a)(x-a)$$

which is true for x close to a.

a. Linear approximation
b. Differentiation of trigonometric functions
c. Smooth function
d. Linearity of differentiation

13. In mathematics, _____ is the process of constructing new data points outside a discrete set of known data points. It is similar to the process of interpolation, which constructs new points between known points, but the results of extrapolations are often less meaningful, and are subject to greater uncertainty. Example illustration of the _____ problem, consisting of assigning a meaningful value at the blue box, at x = 7, given the red data points.

A sound choice of which _____ method to apply relies on a prior knowledge of the process that created the existing data points.

a. ALGOR
b. ACTRAN
c. AUSM
d. Extrapolation

14. A _____ or logistic curve is the most common sigmoid curve. It models the S-curve of growth of some set P, where P might be thought of as population. The initial stage of growth is approximately exponential; then, as saturation begins, the growth slows, and at maturity, growth stops.

a. 15 theorem
b. Logarithmic integral function
c. Multiplication theorem
d. Logistic function

15. The _____ is a polynomial mapping of degree 2, often cited as an archetypal example of how complex, chaotic behaviour can arise from very simple non-linear dynamical equations. The map was popularized in a seminal 1976 paper by the biologist Robert May, in part as a discrete-time demographic model analogous to the logistic equation first created by Pierre François Verhulst. Mathematically, the _____ is written

$$(1) \quad x_{n+1} = rx_n(1 - x_n)$$

where:

x_n is a number between zero and one, and represents the population at year n, and hence x_0 represents the initial population (at year 0)
r is a positive number, and represents a combined rate for reproduction and starvation.

a. 15 theorem
b. BIBO stability
c. BDDC
d. Logistic map

16. In mathematics, the simplest case of _____ refers to the study of problems in which one seeks to minimize or maximize a real function by systematically choosing the values of real or integer variables from within an allowed set. This (a scalar real valued objective function) is actually a small subset of this field which comprises a large area of applied mathematics and generalizes to study of means to obtain 'best available' values of some objective function given a defined domain where the elaboration is on the types of functions and the conditions and nature of the objects in the problem domain.

The first _____ technique, which is known as steepest descent, goes back to Gauss.

a. AUSM
b. ACTRAN
c. ALGOR
d. Optimization

17. In mathematics, the concept of a '_____' is used to describe the behavior of a function as its argument or input either 'gets close' to some point, or as the argument becomes arbitrarily large; or the behavior of a sequence's elements as their index increases indefinitely. Limits are used in calculus and other branches of mathematical analysis to define derivatives and continuity.

In formulas, _____ is usually abbreviated as lim

a. BDDC
b. 15 theorem
c. BIBO stability
d. Limit

Chapter 3. SHORT-CUTS TO DIFFERENTIATION

1. This article will state and prove the _____ for differentiation, and then use it to prove these two formulas.

The _____ for differentiation states that for every natural number n, the derivative of $f(x) = x^n$ is $f'(x) = nx^{n-1}$, that is,

$$(x^n)' = nx^{n-1}.$$

The _____ for integration

$$\int x^n \, dx = \frac{x^{n+1}}{n+1} + C$$

for natural n is then an easy consequence. One just needs to take the derivative of this equality and use the _____ and linearity of differentiation on the right-hand side.

   a. Hyperbolic angle
   b. Power rule
   c. Dirichlet integral
   d. Limits of integration

2. In calculus, a branch of mathematics, the _____ is a measurement of how a function changes when its input changes. Loosely speaking, a _____ can be thought of as how much a quantity is changing at some given point. For example, the _____ of the position (or distance) of a vehicle with respect to time is the instantaneous velocity (respectively, instantaneous speed) at which the vehicle is traveling.

The process of finding a _____ is called differentiation. The fundamental theorem of calculus states that differentiation is the reverse process to integration.

   a. Mountain pass theorem
   b. Ramp function
   c. Concave upwards
   d. Derivative

3. In calculus, _____, was originally the use of expressions such as dx and dy and to represent 'infinitely small' (or infinitesimal) increments of quantities x and y, just as >Δx and >Δy represent finite increments of x and y respectively. So for y being a function of x, or

$$\boxed{x}_>$$

Chapter 3. SHORT-CUTS TO DIFFERENTIATION

the derivative of y with respect to x, which later came to be viewed as

was, according to Leibniz, the quotient of an infinitesimal increment of y by an infinitesimal increment of x, or

where the right hand side is Lagrange's notation for the derivative of f at x.

Similarly, although mathematicians usually now view an integral

as a limit

where >Δx is an interval containing x_i, Leibniz viewed it as the sum (the integral sign denoting summation) of infinitely many infinitesimal quantities f(x) dx.

   a. Fermat differentiation
   b. Notation for differentiation
   c. Leibniz's notation
   d. Gradient

4. The _____ is a function in mathematics. The application of this function to a value x is written as exp(x). Equivalently, this can be written in the form e^x, where e is a mathematical constant, the base of the natural logarithm, which equals approximately 2.718281828, and is also known as Euler's number.
   a. Area hyperbolic functions
   b. ACTRAN
   c. Integral part
   d. Exponential function

Chapter 3. SHORT-CUTS TO DIFFERENTIATION

5. In a totally ordered set all elements are mutually comparable, so such a set can have at most one minimal element and at most one maximal element. Then, due to mutual comparability, the minimal element will also be the least element and the maximal element will also be the greatest element. Thus in a totally ordered set we can simply use the terms minimum and _____.

   a. Dirichlet integral
   b. Hyperbolic angle
   c. Maximum
   d. Complex analysis

6. In calculus, the _____ is a formula for the derivative of the composite of two functions.

   In intuitive terms, if a variable, y, depends on a second variable, u, which in turn depends on a third variable, x, then the rate of change of y with respect to x can be computed as the rate of change of y with respect to u multiplied by the rate of change of u with respect to x. Schematically,

   $$\frac{dy}{dx} = \frac{dy}{du} \cdot \frac{du}{dx}.$$

   a. Differentiation rules
   b. Chain rule
   c. Reciprocal Rule
   d. Quotient Rule

7. In mathematics, a _____ represents the application of one function to the results of another. For instance, the functions f: X → Y and g: Y → Z can be composed by first computing f(x) and then applying a function g to the output of f(x.)

   Thus one obtains a function g ∘ f: X → Z defined by (g ∘ f)(x) = g(f(x)) for all x in X. The notation g ∘ f is read as 'g circle f', or 'g composed with f', 'g after f', 'g following f', or just 'g of f'.

   a. Surjective
   b. Constant function
   c. Range
   d. Composite function

8. In calculus, the _____ is a formula used to find the derivatives of products of functions. It may be stated thus:

   $$(f \cdot g)' = f' \cdot g + f \cdot g'$$

or in the Leibniz notation thus:

$$\frac{d}{dx}(u \cdot v) = u \cdot \frac{dv}{dx} + v \cdot \frac{du}{dx}.$$

Discovery of this rule is credited to Gottfried Leibniz, who demonstrated it using differentials. Here is Leibniz's argument: Let u and v be two differentiable functions of x.

a. Reciprocal Rule
b. Constant factor rule in differentiation
c. Quotient Rule
d. Product rule

9. In mathematics, a _____ of a function of several variables is its derivative with respect to one of those variables with the others held constant (as opposed to the total derivative, in which all variables are allowed to vary.) Partial derivatives are useful in vector calculus and differential geometry.

The _____ of a function f with respect to the variable x is written as f'_x, $\partial_x f$, or $\partial f/\partial x$.

a. Monkey saddle
b. Shift theorem
c. Second partial derivatives test
d. Partial derivative

10. In calculus, the _____ is a method of finding the derivative of a function that is the quotient of two other functions for which derivatives exist.

If the function one wishes to differentiate, f(x), can be written as

$$f(x) = \frac{g(x)}{h(x)}$$

and h(x) ≠ 0, then the rule states that the derivative of g(x) / h(x) is equal to:

$$\frac{d}{dx}f(x) = f'(x) = \frac{g'(x)h(x) - g(x)h'(x)}{[h(x)]^2}.$$

Chapter 3. SHORT-CUTS TO DIFFERENTIATION

Or, more precisely, if all x in some open set containing the number a satisfy h(x) ≠ 0; and g'(a) and h'(a) both exist; then, f'(a) exists as well and:

$$f'(a) = \frac{g'(a)h(a) - g(a)h'(a)}{[h(a)]^2}.$$

The derivative of (4x − 2) / (x² + 1) is:

$$\frac{d}{dx}\left[\frac{(4x-2)}{x^2+1}\right] = \frac{(x^2+1)(4) - (4x-2)(2x)}{(x^2+1)^2}$$
$$= \frac{(4x^2+4) - (8x^2-4x)}{(x^2+1)^2} = \frac{-4x^2+4x+4}{(x^2+1)^2}$$

In the example above, the choices

g(x) = 4x − 2
h(x) = x² + 1

were made. Analogously, the derivative of sin(x) / x² (when x ≠ 0) is:

$$\frac{\cos(x)x^2 - \sin(x)2x}{x^4}$$

Another example is:

$$f(x) = \frac{2x^2}{x^3}$$

whereas g(x) = 2x² and h(x) = x³, and g'(x) = 4x and h'(x) = 3x².

a. Reciprocal Rule
b. Product rule
c. Differentiation rules
d. Quotient rule

11. In mathematics, a _____ is a function that repeats its values in regular intervals or periods. The most important examples are the trigonometric functions, which repeat over intervals of length 2π. Periodic functions are used throughout science to describe oscillations, waves, and other phenomena that exhibit periodicity.

a. Test for Divergence
b. Nth term
c. Term test
d. Periodic function

12. In mathematics, a (topological) _____ is defined as follows: let I be an interval of real numbers (i.e. a non-empty connected subset of $\mathbb{R}$); then a _____ γ is a continuous mapping $\gamma : I \to X$, where X is a topological space. The _____ γ is said to be simple if it is injective, i.e. if for all x, y in I, we have $\gamma(x) = \gamma(y) \implies x = y$. If I is a closed bounded interval $[a, b]$, we also allow the possibility $\gamma(a) = \gamma(b)$ (this convention makes it possible to talk about closed simple _____.)
  a. Curve
  b. Closed curve
  c. Tractrix
  d. Prolate cycloid

13. A _____ in biology generally concerns a measured property such as population size, body height or biomass. Values for the measured property can be plotted on a graph as a function of time.
  a. Separation of variables
  b. Growth curve
  c. Laser diode rate equations
  d. Picone identity

Chapter 4. USING THE DERIVATIVE

1. In mathematics, a _____ is a function which preserves the given order. This concept first arose in calculus, and was later generalized to the more abstract setting of order theory.

In calculus, a function f defined on a subset of the real numbers with real values is called monotonic (also monotonically increasing or non-decreasing), if for all x and y such that x >≤ y one has f(x) >≤ f(y), so f preserves the order.

  a. Pseudo-differential operator
  b. Monotonic function
  c. 15 theorem
  d. Pettis integral

2. In calculus, a branch of mathematics, the _____ is a measurement of how a function changes when its input changes. Loosely speaking, a _____ can be thought of as how much a quantity is changing at some given point. For example, the _____ of the position (or distance) of a vehicle with respect to time is the instantaneous velocity (respectively, instantaneous speed) at which the vehicle is traveling.

The process of finding a _____ is called differentiation. The fundamental theorem of calculus states that differentiation is the reverse process to integration.

  a. Ramp function
  b. Concave upwards
  c. Mountain pass theorem
  d. Derivative

3. In mathematics, a _____ (or critical number) is a point on the domain of a function where:

  - one dimension: the derivative (or slope of the line when visualized) is equal to zero or a point where the function ceases to be differentiable.
  - in general: there are two distinct concepts: either the derivative (Jacobian) vanishes, or it is not of full rank (or, in either case, the function is not differentiable); these agree in one dimension.

Note that in one dimension, a critical value or critical number x of function f is the domain element at which the derivative is zero or undefined, whereas the associated ordered pair (x, y) is the _____. In higher dimensions a critical value is in the range whereas a _____ is in the domain.

There are two situations in which a point becomes a _____ of a function of one variable. The first of which is that the value of the first derivative is equal to zero.

28　　　　　　　　　　　　　Chapter 4. USING THE DERIVATIVE

   a. Critical point
   b. Differentiation operator
   c. Differential operator
   d. Shift theorem

4. In differential topology, a _____ of a differentiable function between differentiable manifolds is the image of a critical point.

The basic result on critical values is Sard's lemma. The set of critical values can be quite irregular; but in Morse theory it becomes important to consider real-valued functions on a manifold M, such that the set of critical values is in fact finite.

   a. Solenoidal
   b. Dispersive partial differential equation
   c. Bloch space
   d. Critical value

5. In calculus, the _____ determines whether a given critical point of a function is a maximum, a minimum, or neither.

Suppose that f is a function and we want to determine if f has a maximum or minimum at x. If f is increasing to the left of x and decreasing to the right of x, then x is a local maximum of f.

   a. Test for Divergence
   b. Hyperbolic angle
   c. Functional integration
   d. First derivative test

6. In calculus, _____, was originally the use of expressions such as dx and dy and to represent 'infinitely small' (or infinitesimal) increments of quantities x and y, just as >Δx and >Δy represent finite increments of x and y respectively. So for y being a function of x, or

> [x] >

the derivative of y with respect to x, which later came to be viewed as

> [x] >

Chapter 4. USING THE DERIVATIVE

was, according to Leibniz, the quotient of an infinitesimal increment of y by an infinitesimal increment of x, or

где the right hand side is Lagrange's notation for the derivative of f at x.

Similarly, although mathematicians usually now view an integral

as a limit

where >Δx is an interval containing x_i, Leibniz viewed it as the sum (the integral sign denoting summation) of infinitely many infinitesimal quantities f(x) dx.

a. Leibniz's notation
b. Gradient
c. Fermat differentiation
d. Notation for differentiation

7. Let f be a differentiable function, and let f'(x) be its derivative. The derivative of f'(x) (if it has one) is written f''(x) and is called the _____ of f. Similarly, the derivative of a _____, if it exists, is written f'''(x) and is called the third derivative of f.
    a. Second derivative
    b. Stationary phase approximation
    c. Ramp function
    d. Horizontal asymptote

8. In calculus, a branch of mathematics, the _____ is a criterion often useful for determining whether a given stationary point of a function is a local maximum or a local minimum.

Chapter 4. USING THE DERIVATIVE

The test states: If the function f is twice differentiable at a stationary point x, meaning that $f'(x) = 0$, then:

- If $f''(x) < 0$ then f has a local maximum at x.
- If $f''(x) > 0$ then f has a local minimum at x.
- If $f''(x) = 0$, the _____ says nothing about the point x, has a possible inflection point.

In the last case, the function may have a local maximum or minimum there, but the function is sufficiently 'flat' that this is undetected by the second derivative. In this case one has to examine the third derivative. Such an example is f(x) = x⁴.

a. Parametric derivative
b. Second derivative test
c. Metric derivative
d. Stationary point

9. In differential calculus, an inflection point, or _____ (or inflexion) is a point on a curve at which the curvature changes sign. The curve changes from being concave upwards (positive curvature) to concave downwards (negative curvature), or vice versa. If one imagines driving a vehicle along the curve, it is a point at which the steering-wheel is momentarily 'straight', being turned from left to right or vice versa.

a. Second derivative test
b. Reduced derivative
c. Linearity of differentiation
d. Point of inflection

10. In mathematics, the simplest case of _____ refers to the study of problems in which one seeks to minimize or maximize a real function by systematically choosing the values of real or integer variables from within an allowed set. This (a scalar real valued objective function) is actually a small subset of this field which comprises a large area of applied mathematics and generalizes to study of means to obtain 'best available' values of some objective function given a defined domain where the elaboration is on the types of functions and the conditions and nature of the objects in the problem domain.

The first _____ technique, which is known as steepest descent, goes back to Gauss.

a. Optimization
b. AUSM
c. ALGOR
d. ACTRAN

11. In mathematics, a (topological) _____ is defined as follows: let I be an interval of real numbers (i.e. a non-empty connected subset of $\mathbb{R}$); then a _____ γ is a continuous mapping $\gamma : I \to X$, where X is a topological space. The _____ γ is said to be simple if it is injective, i.e. if for all x, y in I, we have $\gamma(x) = \gamma(y) \implies x = y$. If I is a closed bounded interval $[a, b]$, we also allow the possibility $\gamma(a) = \gamma(b)$ (this convention makes it possible to talk about closed simple _____.)

a. Curve
b. Closed curve
c. Prolate cycloid
d. Tractrix

12. In economics, the _____ functional form of production functions is widely used to represent the relationship of an output to inputs. It was proposed by Knut Wicksell (1851-1926), and tested against statistical evidence by Charles Cobb and Paul Douglas in 1900-1928.

For production, the function is

Y = AL$^\alpha$K$^\beta$,

where:

- Y = total production (the monetary value of all goods produced in a year)
- L = labor input
- K = capital input
- A = total factor productivity
- α and β are the output elasticities of labor and capital, respectively. These values are constants determined by available technology.

Output elasticity measures the responsiveness of output to a change in levels of either labor or capital used in production, ceteris paribus. For example if α = 0.15, a 1% increase in labor would lead to approximately a 0.15% increase in output.

a. BDDC
b. 15 theorem
c. Cobb-Douglas
d. BIBO stability

13. A _____ or logistic curve is the most common sigmoid curve. It models the S-curve of growth of some set P, where P might be thought of as population. The initial stage of growth is approximately exponential; then, as saturation begins, the growth slows, and at maturity, growth stops.

a. Multiplication theorem
b. Logarithmic integral function
c. 15 theorem
d. Logistic function

14. The _____ is a polynomial mapping of degree 2, often cited as an archetypal example of how complex, chaotic behaviour can arise from very simple non-linear dynamical equations. The map was popularized in a seminal 1976 paper by the biologist Robert May, in part as a discrete-time demographic model analogous to the logistic equation first created by Pierre François Verhulst. Mathematically, the _____ is written

$$(1) \quad x_{n+1} = r x_n (1 - x_n)$$

where:

x_n is a number between zero and one, and represents the population at year n, and hence x_0 represents the initial population (at year 0)
r is a positive number, and represents a combined rate for reproduction and starvation.

a. BDDC
b. BIBO stability
c. 15 theorem
d. Logistic map

Chapter 5. ACCUMULATED CHANGE: THE DEFINITE INTEGRAL

1. Integration is an important concept in mathematics, specifically in the field of calculus and, more broadly, mathematical analysis. Given a function f of a real variable x and an interval [a, b] of the real line, the _____

$$\int_a^b f(x)\, dx,$$

is defined informally to be the net signed area of the region in the xy-plane bounded by the graph of f, the x-axis, and the vertical lines x = a and x = b.

The term '_____' may also refer to the notion of antiderivative, a function F whose derivative is the given function f.

a. Indefinite integral
b. Integral
c. Integral test for convergence
d. Integrand

2. In physics, _____ is defined as the rate of change of position. it is vector physical quantity; both speed and direction are required to define it. In the SI (metric) system, it is measured in meters per second: (m/s) or ms^{-1}.

a. 15 theorem
b. Velocity
c. BIBO stability
d. BDDC

3. In mathematics, the concept of a '_____' is used to describe the behavior of a function as its argument or input either 'gets close' to some point, or as the argument becomes arbitrarily large; or the behavior of a sequence's elements as their index increases indefinitely. Limits are used in calculus and other branches of mathematical analysis to define derivatives and continuity.

In formulas, _____ is usually abbreviated as lim

a. Limit
b. BDDC
c. 15 theorem
d. BIBO stability

4. _____ is the addition of a set of numbers; the result is their sum or total. An interim or present total of a _____ process is termed the running total. The 'numbers' to be summed may be natural numbers, complex numbers, matrices, or still more complicated objects.

a. 15 theorem
b. Summation
c. BIBO stability
d. BDDC

5. In calculus and mathematical analysis the _____ of the integral

$$\int_a^b f(x)\,dx$$

of a Riemann integrable function f defined on a closed and bounded interval [a, b] are the real numbers a and b.

_____ can also be defined for improper integrals, with the _____ of both

$$\lim_{z \to a^+} \int_z^b f(x)\,dx$$

and

$$\lim_{z \to b^-} \int_a^z f(x)\,dx$$

again being a and b. For an improper integral

$$\int_a^\infty f(x)\,dx$$

or

$$\int_{-\infty}^b f(x)\,dx$$

the _____ are a and ∞, or −∞ and b, respectively.

a. Term test
b. Racetrack principle
c. Limits of integration
d. Nth term

Chapter 5. ACCUMULATED CHANGE: THE DEFINITE INTEGRAL

6. In mathematics, a _____ is a method for approximating the total area underneath a curve on a graph, otherwise known as an integral. It may also be used to define the integration operation.

Consider a function $f: D \rightarrow \mathbf{R}$, where D is a subset of the real numbers $\mathbf{R}$, and let $I = [a, b]$ be a closed interval contained in D. A finite set of points $\{x_0, x_1, x_2, ... x_n\}$ such that $a = x_0 < x_1 < x_2 ... < x_n = b$ creates a partition

$$P = \{[x_0, x_1), [x_1, x_2), ... [x_{n-1}, x_n]\}$$

of I.

a. Riemann sum
b. Disk integration
c. Signed measure
d. Surface of revolution

7. In calculus, an _____ is the limit of a definite integral as an endpoint of the interval of integration approaches either a specified real number or ∞ or −∞ or, in some cases, as both endpoints approach limits.

Specifically, an _____ is a limit of the form

$$\lim_{b \to \infty} \int_a^b f(x)\, dx, \qquad \lim_{a \to -\infty} \int_a^b f(x)\, dx,$$

or of the form

$$\lim_{c \to b^-} \int_a^c f(x)\, dx, \qquad \lim_{c \to a^+} \int_c^b f(x)\, dx,$$

in which one takes a limit in one or the other (or sometimes both) endpoints. Improper integrals may also occur at an interior point of the domain of integration, or at multiple such points.

a. AUSM
b. ALGOR
c. Improper integral
d. ACTRAN

Chapter 5. ACCUMULATED CHANGE: THE DEFINITE INTEGRAL

8. In mathematics, a (topological) _____ is defined as follows: let I be an interval of real numbers (i.e. a non-empty connected subset of $\mathbb{R}$); then a _____ γ is a continuous mapping $\gamma : I \to X$, where X is a topological space. The _____ γ is said to be simple if it is injective, i.e. if for all x, y in I, we have $\gamma(x) = \gamma(y) \implies x = y$. If I is a closed bounded interval $[a, b]$, we also allow the possibility $\gamma(a) = \gamma(b)$ (this convention makes it possible to talk about closed simple _____.)

   a. Tractrix
   b. Prolate cycloid
   c. Closed curve
   d. Curve

9. If a function has an integral, it is said to be integrable. The function for which the integral is calculated is called the _____. The region over which a function is being integrated is called the domain of integration.

   a. Order of integration
   b. Integral test for convergence
   c. Integration by parts
   d. Integrand

10. The _____ specifies the relationship between the two central operations of calculus, differentiation and integration.

    The first part of the theorem, sometimes called the first _____, shows that an indefinite integration can be reversed by a differentiation.

    The second part, sometimes called the second _____, allows one to compute the definite integral of a function by using any one of its infinitely many antiderivatives.

    a. Calculus controversy
    b. Minimum
    c. Partial sum
    d. Fundamental Theorem of Calculus

11. In mathematics, especially vector calculus and differential topology, a _____ is a differential form α whose differential is zero (dα = 0), and an exact form is a differential form that is the differential of another differential form β, a 'potential form' or 'primitive' for α, (α = dβ for some differential form β of one-step lower order. Since d² = 0, β is not unique, but can be modified by the addition of the differential of a two-step-lower-order form. This is called gauge transformation.)

a. Soldering
b. Hodge dual
c. Closed form
d. Two-form

Chapter 6. USING THE DEFINITE INTEGRAL

1. In calculus, an _____, primitive or indefinite integral of a function f is a function F whose derivative is equal to f, i.e., F >' = f. The process of solving for antiderivatives is antidifferentiation (or indefinite integration.) Antiderivatives are related to definite integrals through the fundamental theorem of calculus: the definite integral of a function over an interval is equal to the difference between the values of an _____ evaluated at the endpoints of the interval.
    a. Order of integration
    b. Indefinite integral
    c. Integrand
    d. Antiderivative

Chapter 7. ANTIDERIVATIVES

1. In calculus, an antiderivative, primitive or _____ of a function f is a function F whose derivative is equal to f, i.e., F ' = f. The process of solving for antiderivatives is antidifferentiation (or indefinite integration.) Antiderivatives are related to definite integrals through the fundamental theorem of calculus: the definite integral of a function over an interval is equal to the difference between the values of an antiderivative evaluated at the endpoints of the interval.
    a. Arc length
    b. Integral test for convergence
    c. Integration by parts operator
    d. Indefinite integral

2. Integration is an important concept in mathematics, specifically in the field of calculus and, more broadly, mathematical analysis. Given a function f of a real variable x and an interval [a, b] of the real line, the _____

$$\int_a^b f(x)\, dx,$$

is defined informally to be the net signed area of the region in the xy-plane bounded by the graph of f, the x-axis, and the vertical lines x = a and x = b.

The term '_____' may also refer to the notion of antiderivative, a function F whose derivative is the given function f.

   a. Integral test for convergence
   b. Indefinite integral
   c. Integrand
   d. Integral

3. In calculus, an _____, primitive or indefinite integral of a function f is a function F whose derivative is equal to f, i.e., F >' = f. The process of solving for antiderivatives is antidifferentiation (or indefinite integration.) Antiderivatives are related to definite integrals through the fundamental theorem of calculus: the definite integral of a function over an interval is equal to the difference between the values of an _____ evaluated at the endpoints of the interval.
    a. Order of integration
    b. Indefinite integral
    c. Antiderivative
    d. Integrand

4. In a totally ordered set all elements are mutually comparable, so such a set can have at most one minimal element and at most one maximal element. Then, due to mutual comparability, the minimal element will also be the least element and the maximal element will also be the greatest element. Thus in a totally ordered set we can simply use the terms minimum and _____.

Chapter 7. ANTIDERIVATIVES

a. Dirichlet integral
b. Complex analysis
c. Hyperbolic angle
d. Maximum

5. In calculus, the _____ is a formula for the derivative of the composite of two functions.

In intuitive terms, if a variable, y, depends on a second variable, u, which in turn depends on a third variable, x, then the rate of change of y with respect to x can be computed as the rate of change of y with respect to u multiplied by the rate of change of u with respect to x. Schematically,

$$\frac{dy}{dx} = \frac{dy}{du} \cdot \frac{du}{dx}.$$

a. Reciprocal Rule
b. Quotient Rule
c. Differentiation rules
d. Chain rule

6. In economics, the _____ functional form of production functions is widely used to represent the relationship of an output to inputs. It was proposed by Knut Wicksell (1851-1926), and tested against statistical evidence by Charles Cobb and Paul Douglas in 1900-1928.

For production, the function is

$$Y = AL^\alpha K^\beta,$$

where:

- Y = total production (the monetary value of all goods produced in a year)
- L = labor input
- K = capital input
- A = total factor productivity
- α and β are the output elasticities of labor and capital, respectively. These values are constants determined by available technology.

Output elasticity measures the responsiveness of output to a change in levels of either labor or capital used in production, ceteris paribus. For example if α = 0.15, a 1% increase in labor would lead to approximately a 0.15% increase in output.

Chapter 7. ANTIDERIVATIVES

a. BDDC
b. BIBO stability
c. 15 theorem
d. Cobb-Douglas

7. In mathematics, an _____ is a function built from a finite number of exponentials, logarithms, constants, one variable, and nth roots through composition and combinations using the four elementary operations (+ - × ÷.) The trigonometric functions and their inverses are assumed to be included in the elementary functions by using complex variables and the relations between the trigonometric functions and the exponential and logarithm functions.

Elementary functions are considered a subset of special functions.

a. AUSM
b. Elementary function
c. ALGOR
d. ACTRAN

8. In calculus, _____ is a tool for finding antiderivatives and integrals. Using the fundamental theorem of calculus often requires finding an antiderivative. For this and other reasons, _____ is a relatively important tool for mathematicians.
a. Integration by Substitution
b. Extreme value
c. Odd function
d. Integral of secant cubed

9. In mathematics, a _____ is a function that repeats its values in regular intervals or periods. The most important examples are the trigonometric functions, which repeat over intervals of length 2π. Periodic functions are used throughout science to describe oscillations, waves, and other phenomena that exhibit periodicity.
a. Test for Divergence
b. Periodic function
c. Term test
d. Nth term

10. The _____ specifies the relationship between the two central operations of calculus, differentiation and integration.

The first part of the theorem, sometimes called the first _____, shows that an indefinite integration can be reversed by a differentiation.

The second part, sometimes called the second _____, allows one to compute the definite integral of a function by using any one of its infinitely many antiderivatives.

a. Partial sum
b. Calculus controversy
c. Fundamental theorem of calculus
d. Minimum

11. In calculus, an _____ is the limit of a definite integral as an endpoint of the interval of integration approaches either a specified real number or ∞ or −∞ or, in some cases, as both endpoints approach limits.

Specifically, an _____ is a limit of the form

$$\lim_{b\to\infty} \int_a^b f(x)\,dx, \qquad \lim_{a\to-\infty} \int_a^b f(x)\,dx,$$

or of the form

$$\lim_{c\to b^-} \int_a^c f(x)\,dx, \qquad \lim_{c\to a^+} \int_c^b f(x)\,dx,$$

in which one takes a limit in one or the other (or sometimes both) endpoints . Improper integrals may also occur at an interior point of the domain of integration, or at multiple such points.

a. Improper integral
b. AUSM
c. ACTRAN
d. ALGOR

12. In mathematics, the concept of a '_____' is used to describe the behavior of a function as its argument or input either 'gets close' to some point, or as the argument becomes arbitrarily large; or the behavior of a sequence's elements as their index increases indefinitely. Limits are used in calculus and other branches of mathematical analysis to define derivatives and continuity.

In formulas, _____ is usually abbreviated as lim

a. BIBO stability
b. Limit
c. BDDC
d. 15 theorem

13. In calculus and mathematical analysis the _____ of the integral

$$\int_a^b f(x)\, dx$$

of a Riemann integrable function f defined on a closed and bounded interval [a, b] are the real numbers a and b.

_____ can also be defined for improper integrals, with the _____ of both

$$\lim_{z \to a^+} \int_z^b f(x)\, dx$$

and

$$\lim_{z \to b^-} \int_a^z f(x)\, dx$$

again being a and b. For an improper integral

$$\int_a^\infty f(x)\, dx$$

or

$$\int_{-\infty}^b f(x)\, dx$$

the _____ are a and ∞, or −∞ and b, respectively.

a. Racetrack principle
b. Nth term
c. Term test
d. Limits of integration

14. In vector calculus, the _____ is an operator that measures the magnitude of a vector field's source or sink at a given point; the _____ of a vector field is a (signed) scalar. For example, consider air as it is heated or cooled. The relevant vector field for this example is the velocity of the moving air at a point.

a. Divergence Theorem
b. Triple product
c. Gradient theorem
d. Divergence

Chapter 8. PROBABILITY

1. The _____ of a material is defined as its mass per unit volume. The symbol of _____ is ρ '>rho.)

Mathematically:

$$d = \frac{m}{V}$$

where:

    d is the _____,
    m is the mass,
    V is the volume.

a. Density
b. BIBO stability
c. 15 theorem
d. BDDC

2. In mathematics, a _____ (pdf) is a function that represents a probability distribution in terms of integrals.

Formally, a probability distribution has density f, if f is a non-negative Lebesgue-integrable function $\mathbb{R} \to \mathbb{R}$ such that the probability of the interval [a, b] is given by

$$\int_a^b f(x)\, dx$$

for any two numbers a and b. This implies that the total integral of f must be 1.

a. BDDC
b. BIBO stability
c. 15 theorem
d. Probability density function

3. In probability theory and statistics, the _____ (or expectation value or mean and for continuous random variables with a density function it is the probability density -weighted integral of the possible values.

The term '_____' can be misleading.

a. ACTRAN
b. ALGOR
c. AUSM
d. Expected value

4. The _____ is an important family of continuous probability distributions, applicable in many fields. Each member of the family may be defined by two parameters, location and scale: the mean and variance respectively. The standard _____ is the _____ with a mean of zero and a variance of one.

a. Linear regression
b. Continuous random variable
c. Poisson distribution
d. Normal distribution

5. In mathematics, a (topological) _____ is defined as follows: let I be an interval of real numbers (i.e. a non-empty connected subset of $\mathbb{R}$); then a _____ γ is a continuous mapping $\gamma : I \to X$, where X is a topological space. The _____ γ is said to be simple if it is injective, i.e. if for all x, y in I, we have $\gamma(x) = \gamma(y) \implies x = y$. If I is a closed bounded interval $[a, b]$, we also allow the possibility $\gamma(a) = \gamma(b)$ (this convention makes it possible to talk about closed simple _____.)

a. Prolate cycloid
b. Tractrix
c. Closed curve
d. Curve

6. In statistics, _____ is a simple measure of the variability or dispersion of a data set. A low _____ indicates that all of the data points are very close to the same value (the mean), while high _____ indicates that the data is 'spread out' over a large range of values.

For example, the average height for adult men in the United States is about 70 inches, with a _____ of around 3 inches.

a. Moment
b. Poisson distribution
c. Normal distribution
d. Standard deviation

Chapter 9. FUNCTIONS OF SEVERAL VARIABLES

1. The terms '_____' and 'independent variable' are used in similar but subtly different ways in mathematics and statistics as part of the standard terminology in those subjects. They are used to distinguish between two types of quantities being considered, separating them into those available at the start of a process and those being created by it, where the latter (dependent variables) are dependent on the former (independent variables.)

In traditional calculus, a function is defined as a relation between two terms called variables because their values vary.

   a. BDDC
   b. BIBO stability
   c. 15 theorem
   d. Dependent variable

2. In mathematics, the _____ (or replacement set) of a given function is the set of 'input' values for which the function is defined. For instance, the _____ of cosine would be all real numbers, while the _____ of the square root would be only numbers greater than or equal to 0 (ignoring complex numbers in both cases.) In a representation of a function in a xy Cartesian coordinate system, the _____ is represented on the x axis (or abscissa.)

   a. 15 theorem
   b. BIBO stability
   c. BDDC
   d. Domain

3. The terms 'dependent variable' and '_____' are used in similar but subtly different ways in mathematics and statistics as part of the standard terminology in those subjects. They are used to distinguish between two types of quantities being considered, separating them into those available at the start of a process and those being created by it, where the latter (dependent variables) are dependent on the former (independent variables.)

In traditional calculus, a function is defined as a relation between two terms called variables because their values vary.

   a. Independent variable
   b. ACTRAN
   c. AUSM
   d. ALGOR

4. A _____ of a function of two variables is a curve along which the function has a constant value. In cartography, a _____ (often just called a 'contour') joins points of equal elevation (height) above a given level, such as mean sea level. A contour map is a map illustrated with contour lines, for example a topographic map, which thus shows valleys and hills, and the steepness of slopes.

Chapter 9. FUNCTIONS OF SEVERAL VARIABLES

a. BIBO stability
b. Contour line
c. 15 theorem
d. BDDC

5. In mathematics, a (topological) _____ is defined as follows: let I be an interval of real numbers (i.e. a non-empty connected subset of $\mathbb{R}$); then a _____ γ is a continuous mapping $\gamma : I \to X$, where X is a topological space. The _____ γ is said to be simple if it is injective, i.e. if for all x, y in I, we have $\gamma(x) = \gamma(y) \implies x = y$. If I is a closed bounded interval $[a, b]$, we also allow the possibility $\gamma(a) = \gamma(b)$ (this convention makes it possible to talk about closed simple _____.)

a. Prolate cycloid
b. Curve
c. Tractrix
d. Closed curve

6. The _____ of a material is defined as its mass per unit volume. The symbol of _____ is ρ '>rho.)

Mathematically:

$$d = \frac{m}{V}$$

where:

    d is the _____,
    m is the mass,
    V is the volume.

a. BDDC
b. BIBO stability
c. 15 theorem
d. Density

7. In mathematics, a _____ of a function of several variables is its derivative with respect to one of those variables with the others held constant (as opposed to the total derivative, in which all variables are allowed to vary.) Partial derivatives are useful in vector calculus and differential geometry.

The _____ of a function f with respect to the variable x is written as f'_x, $\partial_x f$, or $\partial f/\partial x$.

Chapter 9. FUNCTIONS OF SEVERAL VARIABLES

a. Second partial derivatives test
b. Shift theorem
c. Partial derivative
d. Monkey saddle

8. In calculus, a branch of mathematics, the _____ is a measurement of how a function changes when its input changes. Loosely speaking, a _____ can be thought of as how much a quantity is changing at some given point. For example, the _____ of the position (or distance) of a vehicle with respect to time is the instantaneous velocity (respectively, instantaneous speed) at which the vehicle is traveling.

The process of finding a _____ is called differentiation. The fundamental theorem of calculus states that differentiation is the reverse process to integration.

a. Mountain pass theorem
b. Ramp function
c. Concave upwards
d. Derivative

9. The function difference divided by the point difference is known as the _____, it is also known as Newton's quotient):

$$\frac{\Delta F(P)}{\Delta P} = \frac{F(P + \Delta P) - F(P)}{\Delta P} = \frac{\nabla F(P + \Delta P)}{\Delta P}.$$

If ΔP is infinitesimal, then the _____ is a derivative, otherwise it is a divided difference:

If $|\Delta P| = iota$: $\quad \dfrac{\Delta F(P)}{\Delta P} = \dfrac{dF(P)}{dP} = F'(P) = G(P);$

If $|\Delta P| > iota$: $\quad \dfrac{\Delta F(P)}{\Delta P} = \dfrac{DF(P)}{DP} = F[P, P + \Delta P].$

Regardless if ΔP is infinitesimal or finite, there is (at least--in the case of the derivative--theoretically) a point range, where the boundaries are P ± (.5)ΔP (depending on the orientation--ΔF(P), δF(P) or ∇F(P)):

LB = Lower Boundary; UB = Upper Boundary;

Chapter 9. FUNCTIONS OF SEVERAL VARIABLES

Anyone familiar with derivatives knows that they can be regarded as functions themselves, harboring their own derivatives. Thus each function is home to sequential degrees ('higher orders') of derivation, or differentiation. This property can be generalized to all difference quotients. As this sequencing requires a corresponding boundary splintering, it is practical to break up the point range into smaller, equi-sized sections, with each section being marked by an intermediary point ('P_i'), where LB = P_0 and UB = P_{A_n}, the nth point, equaling the degree/order:

LB = P_0 = P_0 + $0\Delta_1 P$ = P_{A_n} - $(Åf-0)\Delta_1 P$; P_1 = P_0 + $1\Delta_1 P$ = P_{A_n} - $(Åf-1)\Delta_1 P$; P_2 = P_0 + $2\Delta_1 P$ = P_{A_n} - $(Åf-2)\Delta_1 P$; P_3 = P_0 + $3\Delta_1 P$ = P_{A_n} - $(Åf-3)\Delta_1 P$; ↓↓↓↓ P_{A_n-3} = P_0 + $(Åf-3)\Delta_1 P$ = P_{A_n} - $3\Delta_1 P$; P_{A_n-2} = P_0 + $(Åf-2)\Delta_1 P$ = P_{A_n} - $2\Delta_1 P$; P_{A_n-1} = P_0 + $(Åf-1)\Delta_1 P$ = P_{A_n} - $1\Delta_1 P$; UB = P_{A_n-0} = P_0 + $(Åf-0)\Delta_1 P$ = P_{A_n} - $0\Delta_1 P$ = P_{A_n};

$\Delta P = \Delta_1 P = P_1 - P_0 = P_2 - P_1 = P_3 - P_2 = ...$

   a. Linear approximation
   b. Difference quotient
   c. Point of inflection
   d. Checkpointing schemes

10. Integration is an important concept in mathematics, specifically in the field of calculus and, more broadly, mathematical analysis. Given a function f of a real variable x and an interval [a, b] of the real line, the _____

$$\int_a^b f(x)\,dx,$$

is defined informally to be the net signed area of the region in the xy-plane bounded by the graph of f, the x-axis, and the vertical lines x = a and x = b.

The term '_____' may also refer to the notion of antiderivative, a function F whose derivative is the given function f.

   a. Integral test for convergence
   b. Integrand
   c. Indefinite integral
   d. Integral

11. In mathematics, a _____ is an approximation of a general function using a linear function (more precisely, an affine function.)

Chapter 9. FUNCTIONS OF SEVERAL VARIABLES

Given a differentiable function f of one real variable, Taylor's theorem for n=1 states that

$$f(x) = f(a) + f'(a)(x - a) + R_2$$

where R_2 is the remainder term. The _____ is obtained by dropping the remainder:

$$f(x) \approx f(a) + f'(a)(x - a)$$

which is true for x close to a.

a. Linearity of differentiation
b. Differentiation of trigonometric functions
c. Smooth function
d. Linear approximation

12. If a function has an integral, it is said to be integrable. The function for which the integral is calculated is called the _____. The region over which a function is being integrated is called the domain of integration.

a. Integrand
b. Integral test for convergence
c. Order of integration
d. Integration by parts

13. In economics, the _____ functional form of production functions is widely used to represent the relationship of an output to inputs. It was proposed by Knut Wicksell (1851-1926), and tested against statistical evidence by Charles Cobb and Paul Douglas in 1900-1928.

For production, the function is

$Y = AL^{\alpha}K^{\beta}$,

where:

- Y = total production (the monetary value of all goods produced in a year)
- L = labor input
- K = capital input
- A = total factor productivity
- α and β are the output elasticities of labor and capital, respectively. These values are constants determined by available technology.

Chapter 9. FUNCTIONS OF SEVERAL VARIABLES

Output elasticity measures the responsiveness of output to a change in levels of either labor or capital used in production, ceteris paribus. For example if α = 0.15, a 1% increase in labor would lead to approximately a 0.15% increase in output.

a. 15 theorem
b. Cobb-Douglas
c. BDDC
d. BIBO stability

14. In mathematics, the simplest case of _____ refers to the study of problems in which one seeks to minimize or maximize a real function by systematically choosing the values of real or integer variables from within an allowed set. This (a scalar real valued objective function) is actually a small subset of this field which comprises a large area of applied mathematics and generalizes to study of means to obtain 'best available' values of some objective function given a defined domain where the elaboration is on the types of functions and the conditions and nature of the objects in the problem domain.

The first _____ technique, which is known as steepest descent, goes back to Gauss.

a. ALGOR
b. AUSM
c. ACTRAN
d. Optimization

15. In mathematics, a _____ (or critical number) is a point on the domain of a function where:

- one dimension: the derivative (or slope of the line when visualized) is equal to zero or a point where the function ceases to be differentiable.
- in general: there are two distinct concepts: either the derivative (Jacobian) vanishes, or it is not of full rank (or, in either case, the function is not differentiable); these agree in one dimension.

Note that in one dimension, a critical value or critical number x of function f is the domain element at which the derivative is zero or undefined, whereas the associated ordered pair (x, y) is the _____. In higher dimensions a critical value is in the range whereas a _____ is in the domain.

There are two situations in which a point becomes a _____ of a function of one variable. The first of which is that the value of the first derivative is equal to zero.

a. Critical point
b. Differentiation operator
c. Differential operator
d. Shift theorem

16. Let f be a differentiable function, and let f'(x) be its derivative. The derivative of f'(x) (if it has one) is written f''(x) and is called the _____ of f. Similarly, the derivative of a _____, if it exists, is written f'''(x) and is called the third derivative of f.

a. Stationary phase approximation
b. Ramp function
c. Horizontal asymptote
d. Second derivative

17. In calculus, a branch of mathematics, the _____ is a criterion often useful for determining whether a given stationary point of a function is a local maximum or a local minimum.

The test states: If the function f is twice differentiable at a stationary point x, meaning that $f'(x) = 0$, then:

- If $f''(x) < 0$ then f has a local maximum at x.
- If $f''(x) > 0$ then f has a local minimum at x.
- If $f''(x) = 0$, the _____ says nothing about the point x, has a possible inflection point.

In the last case, the function may have a local maximum or minimum there, but the function is sufficiently 'flat' that this is undetected by the second derivative. In this case one has to examine the third derivative. Such an example is f(x) = x⁴.

a. Stationary point
b. Metric derivative
c. Parametric derivative
d. Second derivative test

18. In mathematical optimization, the method of Lagrange multipliers provides a strategy for finding the maximum/minimum of a function subject to constraints.

For example , consider the optimization problem

$$\text{maximize } f(x,y)$$
$$\text{subject to } g(x,y) = c.$$

We introduce a new variable (λ) called a _____, and study the Lagrange function defined by

$$\Lambda(x,y,\lambda) = f(x,y) - \lambda\Big(g(x,y) - c\Big).$$

If (x,y)‰ is a maximum for the original constrained problem, then there exists a λ such that (x,y,λ)‰ is a stationary point for the Lagrange function (stationary points are those points where the partial derivatives of Λ are zero.) However, not all stationary points yield a solution of the original problem.

a. BDDC
b. BIBO stability
c. 15 theorem
d. Lagrange multiplier

19. The method of _____ or ordinary _____ is used to solve overdetermined systems. _____ is often applied in statistical contexts, particularly regression analysis.

_____ can be interpreted as a method of fitting data. The best fit in the _____ sense is that instance of the model for which the sum of squared residuals has its least value, a residual being the difference between an observed value and the value given by the model.

a. 15 theorem
b. BIBO stability
c. BDDC
d. Least squares

20. In mathematics, a _____ is a constant multiplicative factor of a certain object. For example, in the expression $9x^2$, the _____ of x^2 is 9.

The object can be such things as a variable, a vector, a function, etc.

a. Degree of the polynomial
b. Difference polynomial
c. Leading coefficient
d. Coefficient

Chapter 10. MATHEMATICAL MODELING USING DIFFERENTIAL EQUATIONS

1. In infinitesimal calculus, a _____ is traditionally an infinitesimally small change in a variable. For example, if x is a variable, then a change in the value of x is often denoted Δx (or δx when this change is considered to be small.) The _____ dx represents such a change, but is infinitely small.
   a. Continuous function
   b. Dirichlet integral
   c. Related rates
   d. Differential

2. A _____ is a mathematical equation for an unknown function of one or several variables that relates the values of the function itself and of its derivatives of various orders. they play a prominent role in engineering, physics, economics and other disciplines.

   A simplified real world example of a _____ is modeling the acceleration of a ball falling through the air (considering only gravity and air resistance.)

   a. Structural stability
   b. Differential equation
   c. Petrovsky lacuna
   d. Lax pair

3. A _____ in biology generally concerns a measured property such as population size, body height or biomass. Values for the measured property can be plotted on a graph as a function of time.
   a. Growth curve
   b. Laser diode rate equations
   c. Separation of variables
   d. Picone identity

4. In mathematics, a (topological) _____ is defined as follows: let I be an interval of real numbers (i.e. a non-empty connected subset of $\mathbb{R}$); then a _____ γ is a continuous mapping $\gamma : I \to X$, where X is a topological space. The _____ γ is said to be simple if it is injective, i.e. if for all x, y in I, we have $\gamma(x) = \gamma(y) \implies x = y$. If I is a closed bounded interval $[a, b]$, we also allow the possibility $\gamma(a) = \gamma(b)$ (this convention makes it possible to talk about closed simple _____.)
   a. Tractrix
   b. Closed curve
   c. Prolate cycloid
   d. Curve

Chapter 10. MATHEMATICAL MODELING USING DIFFERENTIAL EQUATIONS

5. In mathematics, a _____ to an ordinary or partial differential equation is a function for which the derivatives appearing in the equation may not all exist but which is nonetheless deemed to satisfy the equation in some precisely defined sense. There are many different definitions of _____, appropriate for different classes of equations. One of the most important is based on the notion of distributions.
   a. Riemann-Hilbert correspondence
   b. Nahm equations
   c. Singular perturbation
   d. Weak solution

6. In mathematics, in the field of differential equations, an initial value problem is an ordinary differential equation together with specified value, called the _____, of the unknown function at a given point in the domain of the solution. In physics or other sciences, modeling a system frequently amounts to solving an initial value problem; in this context, the differential equation is an evolution equation specifying how, given initial conditions, the system will evolve with time.

An initial value problem is a differential equation

$$y'(t) = f(t, y(t)) \quad \text{with} \quad f : \mathbb{R} \times \mathbb{R} \to \mathbb{R}$$

together with a point in the domain of f

$$(t_0, y_0) \in \mathbb{R} \times \mathbb{R},$$

called the _____.

   a. AUSM
   b. ACTRAN
   c. Initial condition
   d. ALGOR

7. In mathematics, in the field of differential equations, an _____ is an ordinary differential equation together with specified value, called the initial condition, of the unknown function at a given point in the domain of the solution. In physics or other sciences, modeling a system frequently amounts to solving an _____; in this context, the differential equation is an evolution equation specifying how, given initial conditions, the system will evolve with time.

An _____ is a differential equation

$$y'(t) = f(t, y(t)) \quad \text{with} \quad f : \mathbb{R} \times \mathbb{R} \to \mathbb{R}$$

together with a point in the domain of f

$$(t_0, y_0) \in \mathbb{R} \times \mathbb{R},$$

called the initial condition.

a. AUSM
b. ACTRAN
c. ALGOR
d. Initial value problem

8. The _____ is a function in mathematics. The application of this function to a value x is written as exp(x). Equivalently, this can be written in the form e^x, where e is a mathematical constant, the base of the natural logarithm, which equals approximately 2.718281828, and is also known as Euler's number.

a. Area hyperbolic functions
b. ACTRAN
c. Integral part
d. Exponential function

9. In mathematics, a _____ (or direction field) is a graphical representation of the solutions of a first-order differential equation. It is achieved without solving the differential equation analytically, and thence it is useful. The representation may be used to qualitatively visualise solutions, or to numerically approximate them.

a. Slope field
b. Fresnel integrals
c. The Method of Mechanical Theorems
d. Standard part function

10. In economics, the _____ functional form of production functions is widely used to represent the relationship of an output to inputs. It was proposed by Knut Wicksell (1851-1926), and tested against statistical evidence by Charles Cobb and Paul Douglas in 1900-1928

For production, the function is

$$Y = AL^\alpha K^\beta,$$

where:

- Y = total production (the monetary value of all goods produced in a year)
- L = labor input
- K = capital input
- A = total factor productivity
- α and β are the output elasticities of labor and capital, respectively. These values are constants determined by available technology.

Output elasticity measures the responsiveness of output to a change in levels of either labor or capital used in production, ceteris paribus. For example if α = 0.15, a 1% increase in labor would lead to approximately a 0.15% increase in output.

a. BDDC
b. BIBO stability
c. 15 theorem
d. Cobb-Douglas

11. In mathematics, an _____ is a generalization for the concept of a function in which the dependent variable has not been given 'explicitly' in terms of the independent variable. To give a function f explicitly is to provide a prescription for determining the output value of the function y in terms of the input value x:

$$y = f(x.)$$

By contrast, the function is implicit if the value of y is obtained from x by solving an equation of the form:

$$R(x,y) = 0.$$

a. Automatic differentiation
b. Implicit function
c. Implicit differentiation
d. Ordinary differential equation

12. _____ is called the proportionality constant or _____.

- If an object travels at a constant speed, then the distance traveled is proportional to the time spent travelling, with the speed being the _____.

- The circumference of a circle is proportional to its diameter, with the _____ equal to π.

- On a map drawn to scale, the distance between any two points on the map is proportional to the distance between the two locations that the points represent, with the _____ being the scale of the map.

- The force acting on a certain object due to gravity is proportional to the object's mass; the _____ between the the mass and the force is known as gravitational acceleration.

Since

$$y = kx$$

is equivalent to

$$x = \left(\frac{1}{k}\right)y,$$

it follows that if y is proportional to x, with (nonzero) proportionality constant k, then x is also proportional to y with proportionality constant 1/k.

If y is proportional to x, then the graph of y as a function of x will be a straight line passing through the origin with the slope of the line equal to the _____: it corresponds to linear growth.

a. BDDC
b. 15 theorem
c. BIBO stability
d. Constant of proportionality

13. In mathematics, _____ is any of several methods for solving ordinary and partial differential equations, in which algebra allows one to rewrite an equation so that each of two variables occurs on a different side of the equation.

Suppose a differential equation can be written in the form

$$\frac{d}{dx}f(x) = g(x)h(f(x)), \qquad (1)$$

which we can write more simply by letting y = f(x):

$$\frac{dy}{dx} = g(x)h(y).$$

As long as h(y) ≠ 0, we can rearrange terms to obtain:

$$\frac{dy}{h(y)} = g(x)dx,$$

so that the two variables x and y have been separated.

Some who dislike Leibniz's notation may prefer to write this as

$$\frac{1}{h(y)}\frac{dy}{dx} = g(x),$$

but that fails to make it quite as obvious why this is called '_____'.

   a. Chebyshev's equation
   b. Characteristic multiplier
   c. Node
   d. Separation of variables

14. _____ is the concept of adding accumulated interest back to the principal, so that interest is earned on interest from that moment on. The act of declaring interest to be principal is called compounding (i.e., interest is compounded.) A loan, for example, may have its interest compounded every month: in this case, a loan with $100 principal and 1% interest per month would have a balance of $101 at the end of the first month.
   a. BIBO stability
   b. Compound interest
   c. BDDC
   d. 15 theorem

15. The _____ are a pair of first order, non-linear, differential equations frequently used to describe the dynamics of biological systems in which two species interact, one a predator and one its prey. They were proposed independently by Alfred J. Lotka in 1925 and Vito Volterra in 1926.

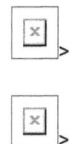

where

- y is the number of some predator;
- x is the number of its prey;
- dy/dt and dx/dt represents the growth of the two populations against time;
- t represents the time; and
- >α, >β, >γ and >δ are parameters representing the interaction of the two species.

When multiplied out, the equations take a form useful for physical interpretation. Their origin should be considered from a more general framework,

where both functions represent per capita growth rates of the prey and predator, respectively.

a. BIBO stability
b. BDDC
c. 15 theorem
d. Lotka-Volterra equations

16. A _____ is a visual display of certain characteristics of certain kinds of differential equations.

Phase planes are useful in visualizing the behavior of physical systems; in particular, of oscillatory systems such as predator-prey models These models can 'spiral in' towards zero, 'spiral out' towards infinity, or reach neutrally stable situations called centres where the path traced out can be either circular, elliptical, or ovoid, or some variant thereof.

a. Phase plane
b. Separation of variables
c. Frobenius method
d. Power series method

Chapter 11. GEOMETRIC SERIES

1. In mathematics, a _____ is a series with a constant ratio between successive terms. For example, the series

$$\frac{1}{2} + \frac{1}{4} + \frac{1}{8} + \frac{1}{16} + \cdots$$

is geometric, because each term is equal to half of the previous term. The sum of this series is 1, as illustrated in the following picture:

_____ are one of the simplest examples of infinite series with finite sums.

   a. Sequence transformation
   b. Converge absolutely
   c. Telescoping series
   d. Geometric series

2. In mathematics, especially vector calculus and differential topology, a _____ is a differential form α whose differential is zero (dα = 0), and an exact form is a differential form that is the differential of another differential form β, a 'potential form' or 'primitive' for α, (α = dβ for some differential form β of one-step lower order. Since d^2 = 0, β is not unique, but can be modified by the addition of the differential of a two-step-lower-order form. This is called gauge transformation.)
   a. Hodge dual
   b. Two-form
   c. Closed form
   d. Soldering

3. Cantor defined two kinds of _____ numbers, the ordinal numbers and the cardinal numbers. Ordinal numbers may be identified with well-ordered sets, or counting carried on to any stopping point, including points after an _____ number have already been counted. Generalizing finite and the ordinary _____ sequences which are maps from the positive integers leads to mappings from ordinal numbers, and transfinite sequences.
   a. ALGOR
   b. ACTRAN
   c. AUSM
   d. Infinite

4. Call S_N the _____ to N of the sequence {a_n}, or _____ of the series. A series is the sequence of partial sums, {S_N}.

Chapter 11. GEOMETRIC SERIES

When talking about series, one can refer either to the sequence $\{S_N\}$ of the partial sums, or to the sum of the series,

$$\sum_{n=0}^{\infty} a_n$$

i.e., the limit of the sequence of partial sums - it is clear which one is meant from context.

a. Periodic function
b. Minimum
c. Root test
d. Partial sum

5. _____ (including exponential decay) occurs when the growth rate of a mathematical function is proportional to the function's current value. In the case of a discrete domain of definition with equal intervals it is also called geometric growth or geometric decay (the function values form a geometric progression.)

_____ is said to follow an exponential law; the simple-_____ model is known as the Malthusian growth model.

a. Exponential growth
b. Inseparable differential equation
c. Oscillating
d. Isomonodromic deformation

6. The _____ is a polynomial mapping of degree 2, often cited as an archetypal example of how complex, chaotic behaviour can arise from very simple non-linear dynamical equations. The map was popularized in a seminal 1976 paper by the biologist Robert May, in part as a discrete-time demographic model analogous to the logistic equation first created by Pierre François Verhulst. Mathematically, the _____ is written

$$(1) \qquad x_{n+1} = r x_n (1 - x_n)$$

where:

x_n is a number between zero and one, and represents the population at year n, and hence x_0 represents the initial population (at year 0)

r is a positive number, and represents a combined rate for reproduction and starvation.

a. BDDC
b. BIBO stability
c. Logistic map
d. 15 theorem

7. A _____ or logistic curve is the most common sigmoid curve. It models the S-curve of growth of some set P, where P might be thought of as population. The initial stage of growth is approximately exponential; then, as saturation begins, the growth slows, and at maturity, growth stops.
a. Logistic function
b. Multiplication theorem
c. Logarithmic integral function
d. 15 theorem

Chapter 1

1. b	2. a	3. a	4. b	5. d	6. c	7. b	8. b	9. d	10. d
11. c	12. d	13. b	14. d	15. b	16. d	17. a	18. d	19. d	20. d
21. d	22. b	23. d	24. d	25. b	26. d	27. d	28. b	29. d	30. d
31. d	32. c	33. c	34. d						

Chapter 2

1. d	2. c	3. d	4. d	5. a	6. d	7. d	8. d	9. d	10. d
11. d	12. a	13. d	14. d	15. d	16. d	17. d			

Chapter 3

1. b	2. d	3. c	4. d	5. c	6. b	7. d	8. d	9. d	10. d
11. d	12. a	13. b							

Chapter 4

1. b	2. d	3. a	4. d	5. d	6. a	7. a	8. b	9. d	10. a
11. a	12. c	13. d	14. d						

Chapter 5

1. b	2. b	3. a	4. b	5. c	6. a	7. c	8. d	9. d	10. d
11. c									

Chapter 6

1. d

Chapter 7

1. d	2. d	3. c	4. d	5. d	6. d	7. b	8. a	9. b	10. c
11. a	12. b	13. d	14. d						

Chapter 8

1. a	2. d	3. d	4. d	5. d	6. d

Chapter 9

1. d	2. d	3. a	4. b	5. b	6. d	7. c	8. d	9. b	10. d
11. d	12. a	13. b	14. d	15. a	16. d	17. d	18. d	19. d	20. d

Chapter 10

1. d	2. b	3. a	4. d	5. d	6. c	7. d	8. d	9. a	10. d
11. b	12. d	13. d	14. b	15. d	16. a				

Chapter 11

1. d	2. c	3. d	4. d	5. a	6. c	7. a

www.ingramcontent.com/pod-product-compliance
Lightning Source LLC
Chambersburg PA
CBHW081219230426
43666CB00015B/2800